C000160620

CHINESE HOROSCOPES FOR LOVERS

The Rabbit

LORI REID

illustrated by

PAUL COLLICUTT

ELEMENT BOOKS

Shaftesbury, Dorset • Rockport, Massachusetts • Brisbane, Queensland

First published in Great Britain in 1996 by

ELEMENT BOOKS LIMITED

Shaftesbury, Dorset SP7 8BP

Published in the USA in 1996 by

ELEMENT BOOKS, INC.

PO Box 830, Rockport, MA 01966

Published in Australia in 1996 by

ELEMENT BOOKS LIMITED

for JACARANDA WILEY LIMITED

33 Park Road, Milton, Brisbane 4064

Designed and created by

THE BRIDGEWATER BOOK COMPANY

Art directed by *Peter Bridgewater*

Designed by *Angela Neal*

Picture research by *Vanessa Fletcher*

Edited by *Gillian Delaforce*

Printed and bound in Great Britain by
BPC Paulton Books Ltd

British Library Cataloguing in Publication data available

Library of Congress Cataloging in Publication data available

ISBN 1-85230-764-1

Contents

Why are some people lucky in love and others not?

Chinese Astrology

SOME PEOPLE fall in love and, as the fairy tales go, live happily ever after. Others fall in love – again and again, make the same mistakes every time and never form a lasting relationship. Most of us come between these two extremes, and some people form remarkably successful unions while others make spectacular disasters of their personal lives. Why are some people lucky in love while others have the odds stacked against them?

ANIMAL NAMES

According to the philosophy of the Far East, luck has very little to do with it. The answer, the philosophers say, lies with 'the Animal that hides in our hearts'. This Animal, of which there are 12, forms part of the complex art of Chinese Astrology. Each year of a 12-year cycle is attributed an Animal sign, whose characteristics are said to influence worldly events as well as the personality and fate of each living thing that comes under its dominion. The 12 Animals run in sequence, beginning with the Rat and followed by the Ox, Tiger, Rabbit, Dragon, Snake, Horse, Sheep, Monkey, Rooster, Dog and last, but not least, the Pig. Being born in the Year of the Ox, for example, is simply a way of describing what you're like, physically and psychologically. And this is quite different from someone who, for instance, is born in the Year of the Snake.

The 12 Animals of Chinese Astrology.

RELATIONSHIPS

These Animal names are merely the tip of the iceberg, considering the complexity of the whole subject. Yet such are the richness and wisdom of Chinese Astrology that understanding the principles behind the year in which you were born will give you powerful insights into your own personality. The system is very specific about which Animals are compatible and which are antagonistic and this tells us whether our relationships will be successful. Marriages are made in heaven, so the saying goes. The heavens, according to Chinese beliefs, can point the way. The rest is up to us.

Year Chart and Birth Dates

UNLIKE THE WESTERN CALENDAR, which is based on the Sun, the Oriental year is based on the movement of the Moon, which means that New Year's Day does not fall on a fixed date. This Year Chart, taken from the Chinese Perpetual Calendar, lists the dates on which each year begins and ends together with its Animal ruler for the year. In addition, the Chinese believe that the tangible world is composed of 5 elements, each slightly adapting the characteristics of the Animal signs. These elemental influences are also given here. Finally, the aspect, that is, whether the year is characteristically Yin (-) or Yang (+), is also listed.

The Western calendar is based on the Sun; the Oriental on the Moon.

YIN AND YANG

Yin and Yang are the terms given to the dynamic complementary forces that keep the universe in balance and which are the central principles behind life. Yin is all that is considered negative, passive, feminine, night, the Moon, while Yang is considered positive, active, masculine, day, the Sun.

Year	From – To	Animal sign	Element	Aspect
1900	31 Jan 1900 – 18 Feb 1901	Rat	Metal	+ Yang
1901	19 Feb 1901 – 7 Feb 1902	Ox	Metal	– Yin
1902	8 Feb 1902 – 28 Jan 1903	Tiger	Water	+ Yang
1903	29 Jan 1903 – 15 Feb 1904	Rabbit	Water	– Yin
1904	16 Feb 1904 – 3 Feb 1905	Dragon	Wood	+ Yang
1905	4 Feb 1905 – 24 Jan 1906	Snake	Wood	– Yin
1906	25 Jan 1906 – 12 Feb 1907	Horse	Fire	+ Yang
1907	13 Feb 1907 – 1 Feb 1908	Sheep	Fire	– Yin
1908	2 Feb 1908 – 21 Jan 1909	Monkey	Earth	+ Yang
1909	22 Jan 1909 – 9 Feb 1910	Rooster	Earth	– Yin
1910	10 Feb 1910 – 29 Jan 1911	Dog	Metal	+ Yang
1911	30 Jan 1911 – 17 Feb 1912	Pig	Metal	– Yin
1912	18 Feb 1912 – 5 Feb 1913	Rat	Water	+ Yang
1913	6 Feb 1913 – 25 Jan 1914	Ox	Water	– Yin
1914	26 Jan 1914 – 13 Feb 1915	Tiger	Wood	+ Yang
1915	14 Feb 1915 – 2 Feb 1916	Rabbit	Wood	– Yin
1916	3 Feb 1916 – 22 Jan 1917	Dragon	Fire	+ Yang
1917	23 Jan 1917 – 10 Feb 1918	Snake	Fire	– Yin
1918	11 Feb 1918 – 31 Jan 1919	Horse	Earth	+ Yang
1919	1 Feb 1919 – 19 Feb 1920	Sheep	Earth	– Yin
1920	20 Feb 1920 – 7 Feb 1921	Monkey	Metal	+ Yang
1921	8 Feb 1921 – 27 Jan 1922	Rooster	Metal	– Yin
1922	28 Jan 1922 – 15 Feb 1923	Dog	Water	+ Yang
1923	16 Feb 1923 – 4 Feb 1924	Pig	Water	– Yin
1924	5 Feb 1924 – 24 Jan 1925	Rat	Wood	+ Yang
1925	25 Jan 1925 – 12 Feb 1926	Ox	Wood	– Yin
1926	13 Feb 1926 – 1 Feb 1927	Tiger	Fire	+ Yang
1927	2 Feb 1927 – 22 Jan 1928	Rabbit	Fire	– Yin
1928	23 Jan 1928 – 9 Feb 1929	Dragon	Earth	+ Yang
1929	10 Feb 1929 – 29 Jan 1930	Snake	Earth	– Yin
1930	30 Jan 1930 – 16 Feb 1931	Horse	Metal	+ Yang
1931	17 Feb 1931 – 5 Feb 1932	Sheep	Metal	– Yin
1932	6 Feb 1932 – 25 Jan 1933	Monkey	Water	+ Yang
1933	26 Jan 1933 – 13 Feb 1934	Rooster	Water	– Yin
1934	14 Feb 1934 – 3 Feb 1935	Dog	Wood	+ Yang
1935	4 Feb 1935 – 23 Jan 1936	Pig	Wood	– Yin

Year	From – To	Animal sign	Element	Aspect
1936	24 Jan 1936 – 10 Feb 1937	Rat	Fire	+ Yang
1937	11 Feb 1937 – 30 Jan 1938	Ox	Fire	– Yin
1938	31 Jan 1938 – 18 Feb 1939	Tiger	Earth	+ Yang
1939	19 Feb 1939 – 7 Feb 1940	Rabbit	Earth	– Yin
1940	8 Feb 1940 – 26 Jan 1941	Dragon	Metal	+ Yang
1941	27 Jan 1941 – 14 Feb 1942	Snake	Metal	– Yin
1942	15 Feb 1942 – 4 Feb 1943	Horse	Water	+ Yang
1943	5 Feb 1943 – 24 Jan 1944	Sheep	Water	– Yin
1944	25 Jan 1944 – 12 Feb 1945	Monkey	Wood	+ Yang
1945	13 Feb 1945 – 1 Feb 1946	Rooster	Wood	– Yin
1946	2 Feb 1946 – 21 Jan 1947	Dog	Fire	+ Yang
1947	22 Jan 1947 – 9 Feb 1948	Pig	Fire	– Yin
1948	10 Feb 1948 – 28 Jan 1949	Rat	Earth	+ Yang
1949	29 Jan 1949 – 16 Feb 1950	Ox	Earth	– Yin
1950	17 Feb 1950 –5 Feb 1951	Tiger	Metal	+ Yang
1951	6 Feb 1951 – 26 Jan 1952	Rabbit	Metal	– Yin
1952	27 Jan 1952 – 13 Feb 1953	Dragon	Water	+ Yang
1953	14 Feb 1953 – 2 Feb 1954	Snake	Water	– Yin
1954	3 Feb 1954 – 23 Jan 1955	Horse	Wood	+ Yang
1955	24 Jan 1955 – 11 Feb 1956	Sheep	Wood	– Yin
1956	12 Feb 1956 – 30 Jan 1957	Monkey	Fire	+ Yang
1957	31 Jan 1957 – 17 Feb 1958	Rooster	Fire	– Yin
1958	18 Feb 1958 – 7 Feb 1959	Dog	Earth	+ Yang
1959	8 Feb 1959 – 27 Jan 1960	Pig	Earth	– Yin
1960	28 Jan 1960 – 14 Feb 1961	Rat	Metal	+ Yang
1961	15 Feb 1961 – 4 Feb 1962	Ox	Metal	– Yin
1962	5 Feb 1962 – 24 Jan 1963	Tiger	Water	+ Yang
1963	25 Jan 1963 – 12 Feb 1964	Rabbit	Water	– Yin
1964	13 Feb 1964 – 1 Feb 1965	Dragon	Wood	+ Yang
1965	2 Feb 1965 – 20 Jan 1966	Snake	Wood	– Yin
1966	21 Jan 1966 – 8 Feb 1967	Horse	Fire	+ Yang
1967	9 Feb 1967 – 29 Jan 1968	Sheep	Fire	– Yin
1968	30 Jan 1968 – 16 Feb 1969	Monkey	Earth	+ Yang
1969	17 Feb 1969 – 5 Feb 1970	Rooster	Earth	– Yin
1970	6 Feb 1970 – 26 Jan 1971	Dog	Metal	+ Yang
1971	27 Jan 1971 – 15 Jan 1972	Pig	Metal	– Yin

Year	From – To	Animal sign	Element	Aspect	
1972	16 Jan 1972 – 2 Feb 1973	Rat	Water	+	Yang
1973	3 Feb 1973 – 22 Jan 1974	Ox	Water	–	Yin
1974	23 Jan 1974 – 10 Feb 1975	Tiger	Wood	+	Yang
1975	11 Feb 1975 – 30 Jan 1976	Rabbit	Wood	–	Yin
1976	31 Jan 1976 – 17 Feb 1977	Dragon	Fire	+	Yang
1977	18 Feb 1977 – 6 Feb 1978	Snake	Fire	–	Yin
1978	7 Feb 1978 – 27 Jan 1979	Horse	Earth	+	Yang
1979	28 Jan 1979 – 15 Feb 1980	Sheep	Earth	–	Yin
1980	16 Feb 1980 – 4 Feb 1981	Monkey	Metal	+	Yang
1981	5 Feb 1981 – 24 Jan 1982	Rooster	Metal	–	Yin
1982	25 Jan 1982 – 12 Feb 1983	Dog	Water	+	Yang
1983	13 Feb 1983 – 1 Feb 1984	Pig	Water	–	Yin
1984	2 Feb 1984 – 19 Feb 1985	Rat	Wood	+	Yang
1985	20 Feb 1985 – 8 Feb 1986	Ox	Wood	–	Yin
1986	9 Feb 1986 – 28 Jan 1987	Tiger	Fire	+	Yang
1987	29 Jan 1987 – 16 Feb 1988	Rabbit	Fire	–	Yin
1988	17 Feb 1988 – 5 Feb 1989	Dragon	Earth	+	Yang
1989	6 Feb 1989 – 26 Jan 1990	Snake	Earth	–	Yin
1990	27 Jan 1990 – 14 Feb 1991	Horse	Metal	+	Yang
1991	15 Feb 1991 – 3 Feb 1992	Sheep	Metal	–	Yin
1992	4 Feb 1992 – 22 Jan 1993	Monkey	Water	+	Yang
1993	23 Jan 1993 – 9 Feb 1994	Rooster	Water	–	Yin
1994	10 Feb 1994 – 30 Jan 1995	Dog	Wood	+	Yang
1995	31 Jan 1995 – 18 Feb 1996	Pig	Wood	–	Yin
1996	19 Feb 1996 – 7 Feb 1997	Rat	Fire	+	Yang
1997	8 Feb 1997 – 27 Jan 1998	Ox	Fire	–	Yin
1998	28 Jan 1998 – 15 Feb 1999	Tiger	Earth	+	Yang
1999	16 Feb 1999 – 4 Feb 2000	Rabbit	Earth	–	Yin
2000	5 Feb 2000 – 23 Jan 2001	Dragon	Metal	+	Yang
2001	24 Jan 2001 – 11 Feb 2002	Snake	Metal	–	Yin
2002	12 Feb 2002 – 31 Jan 2003	Horse	Water	+	Yang
2003	1 Feb 2003 – 21 Jan 2004	Sheep	Water	–	Yin
2004	22 Jan 2004 – 8 Feb 2005	Monkey	Wood	+	Yang
2005	9 Feb 2005 – 28 Jan 2006	Rooster	Wood	–	Yin
2006	29 Jan 2006 – 17 Feb 2007	Dog	Fire	+	Yang
2007	18 Feb 2007 – 6 Feb 2008	Pig	Fire	–	Yin

Introducing the Animals

THE RAT  ♥ ♥ ♥ DRAGON, MONKEY ✖ HORSE

Outwardly cool, Rats are passionate lovers with depths of feeling that others don't often recognize. Rats are very self-controlled.

THE OX  ♥ ♥ ♥ SNAKE, ROOSTER ✖ SHEEP

Not necessarily the most romantic of the signs, Ox people make steadfast lovers as well as faithful, affectionate partners.

THE TIGER  ♥ ♥ ♥ HORSE, DOG ✖ MONKEY

Passionate and sensual, Tigers are exciting lovers. Flirty when young, once committed they make stable partners and keep their sexual allure.

THE RABBIT  ♥ ♥ ♥ SHEEP, PIG ✖ ROOSTER

Gentle, emotional and sentimental, Rabbits make sensitive lovers. They are shrewd and seek a partner who offers security.

THE DRAGON ♥ ♥ ♥ RAT, MONKEY ✖ DOG

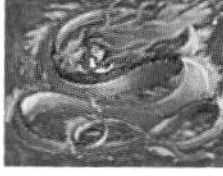

Dragon folk get as much stimulation from mind-touch as they do through sex. A partner on the same wave-length is essential.

THE SNAKE ♥ ♥ ♥ OX, ROOSTER ✖ PIG

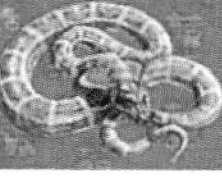

Deeply passionate, strongly sexed but not aggressive, snakes are attracted to elegant, refined partners. But they are deeply jealous and possessive.

♥ ♥ ♥ *COMPATIBLE* ✖ *INCOMPATIBLE*

THE HORSE ♥ ♥ ♥ TIGER, DOG ✖ RAT

For horse-born folk love is blind. In losing their hearts, they lose their heads and make several mistakes before finding the right partner.

THE SHEEP ♥ ♥ ♥ RABBIT, PIG ✖ OX

Sheep-born people are made for marriage. Domesticated home-lovers, they find emotional satisfaction with a partner who provides security.

THE MONKEY ♥ ♥ ♥ DRAGON, RAT ✖ TIGER

Clever and witty, Monkeys need partners who will keep them stimulated. Forget the 9 to 5 routine, these people need *pizzazz.*

THE ROOSTER ♥ ♥ ♥ OX, SNAKE ✖ RABBIT

The Rooster's stylish good looks guarantee they will attract many suitors. They are level-headed and approach relationships coolly.

THE DOG ♥ ♥ ♥ TIGER, HORSE ✖ DRAGON

A loving, stable relationship is an essential component in the lives of Dogs. Once they have found their mate, they remain faithful for life.

THE PIG ♥ ♥ ♥ RABBIT, SHEEP ✖ SNAKE

These are sensual hedonists who enjoy lingering love-making between satin sheets. Caviar and champagne go down very nicely too.

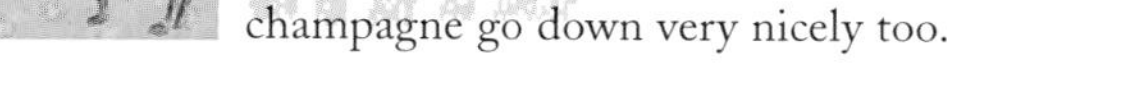

兔

The Rabbit Personality

YEARS OF THE RABBIT

1903 ★ 1915 ★ 1927 ★ 1939 ★ 1951 ★ 1963

1975 ★ 1987 ★ 1999

RABBIT FOLK are quiet, private individuals, sensitive and shy. Being born into this sign means that you tend to shun the limelight, preferring to take a behind-the-scenes, rather than a high-profile, approach to life. It's not that you're reclusive. In fact, quite the reverse. You're a very social creature, enjoying a good chat and the company of others. It's simply that you're comfortable being just one of the crowd.

RABBIT FACTS

Fourth in order ★ *Chinese name – TU* ★ *Sign of Peace* ★ *Hour 5AM–6.59AM* ★ *Month – March* ★ *Western counterpart – Pisces* ★

CHARACTERISTICS

♥ *Wisdom* ♥ *Astuteness* ♥ *Prescience* ♥ *Docility* ♥ *Thoughtfulness* ♥ *Refinement*

✖ *Cunning* ✖ *Possessiveness* ✖ *Fussiness* ✖ *Obsession* ✖ *Snobbery*

SIGN OF PEACE

Yours is the sign of peace so you're the least aggressive of the Chinese Animals. You are born with an inbuilt gift for diplomacy which enables you to extricate yourself with tact from any potentially troublesome situation. To be a good diplomat requires intelligence and psychological penetration. It also requires powers of persuasion and cunning. Rabbits are masters and mistresses of such finesse!

Rabbits are highly cultured, with a strong artistic vein.

RABBIT STYLE

The Chinese Rabbit is synonymous with style and culture. Chic and sophisticated, you look as if you've just stepped out of the pages of *Vogue*. Your artistic vein means that Rabbits dominate the world of music and the Arts.

兔

Your Hour of Birth

WHILE YOUR YEAR OF BIRTH describes your fundamental character, the Animal governing the actual hour in which you were born describes your outer temperament, how people see you or the picture you present to the outside world. Note that each Animal rules over two consecutive hours. Also note that these are GMT standard times and that adjustments need to be made if you were born during Summer or daylight saving time.

11PM – 12.59AM ★ RAT

Pleasant, sociable, easy to get on with. An active, confident, busy person – and a bit of a busybody to boot.

1AM – 2.59AM ★ OX

Level-headed and down-to-earth, you come across as knowledgeable and reliable – sometimes, though, a bit biased.

3AM – 4.59AM ★ TIGER

Enthusiastic and self-assured, people see you as a strong and positive personality – at times a little over-exuberant.

5AM – 6.59AM ★ RABBIT

You're sensitive and shy and don't project your real self to the world. You feel you have to put on an act to please others.

7AM – 8.59AM ★ DRAGON

Independent and interesting, you present a picture of someone who is quite out of the ordinary.

9AM – 10.59AM ★ SNAKE

You can be a bit difficult to fathom and, because you appear so controlled, people either take to you instantly, or not at all.

11AM – 12.59PM ★ HORSE

Open, cheerful and happy-go-lucky is the picture you always put across to others. You're an extrovert and it generally shows.

1PM – 2.59PM ★ SHEEP

Your unassuming nature won't allow you to foist yourself upon others so people see you as quiet and retiring – but eminently sensible, though.

3PM – 4.59PM ★ MONKEY

Lively and talkative, that twinkle in your eye will guarantee you make friends wherever you go.

5PM – 6.59PM ★ ROOSTER

There's something rather stylish in your approach that gives people an impression of elegance and glamour. But you don't suffer fools gladly.

7PM – 8.59PM ★ DOG

Some people see you as steady and reliable, others as quiet and graceful and others still as dull and unimaginative. It all depends who you're with at the time.

9PM – 10.59PM ★ PIG

Your laid-back manner conceals a depth of interest and intelligence that doesn't always come through at first glance.

Your hour of birth describes your outer temperament.

The Rabbit Lover

As a lover, you have a tendency to 'mother' your partner which can become 'smothering', if it develops into possessiveness, but you are considerate and accommodating.

BECAUSE RABBIT-BORN people are such dichotomous creatures, the saying, 'Never judge a book by its cover' is aptly applied to you. You wouldn't dream of wearing your heart on your sleeve, you're aloof, yet underneath you're sensual and loving. Your tough façade protects a tender interior. You're romantic yet realistic, generous yet mercenary. Rabbits are strongly Yin and, whether male or female, are in tune with the feminine part of their psyche. Your mothering instinct compels you to nurture others and you have an innate love of home and family.

Behind the tough Rabbit facade lies a romantic nature.

YIN DOMINANCE

It's part of the Yin dominance that brings out a prevalent sentimentality in your nature. Soft, romantic and nostalgic, you're easily moved and at times it's difficult for you to hold back the

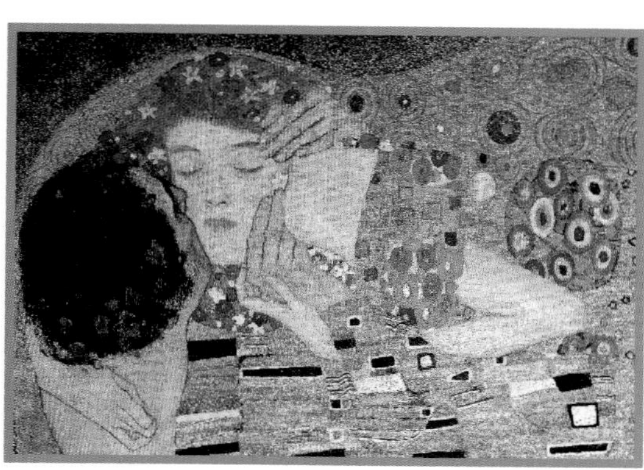

The Kiss
GUSTAV KLIMT 1862–1918

tears. You're prone to mood swings, too, since you're easily influenced by the company you keep and the environment you find yourself in. The merest hint of confrontation will send you to bed clutching an ice-pack and a bottle of aspirin.

SUAVE AND SLEEK

Belonging to this sign means you're beautiful, charming and genteel. Suave and sophisticated or sleek and refined, anyone would consider you an asset to have by his or her side. However, despite your cool, dignified demeanour, Rabbit folk have a well-earned reputation for being highly sexed. Though you may sow a few wild oats when young, most of you, once committed, tend to remain with your chosen partner for life.

Rabbits are sleek and sophisticated.

In Your Element

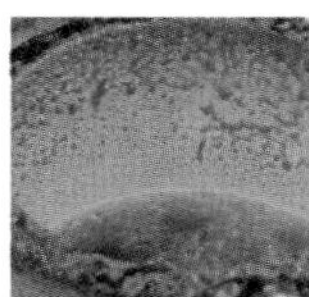

ALTHOUGH YOUR SIGN recurs every 12 years, each generation is slightly modified by one of 5 elements. If you were born under the Metal influence your character, emotions and behaviour would show significant variations from an individual born under one of the other elements. Check the Year Chart for your ruling element and discover what effects it has upon you.

THE METAL RABBIT ★ 1951

Metal gives you a much stronger presence, more resilience and tenacity than the average, often timid, Rabbit. Strongly intuitive, you can be shrewd, even cunning, in your dealings. Your feelings run deep and love affairs can become intense. Metal Rabbits are highly accomplished in the Arts.

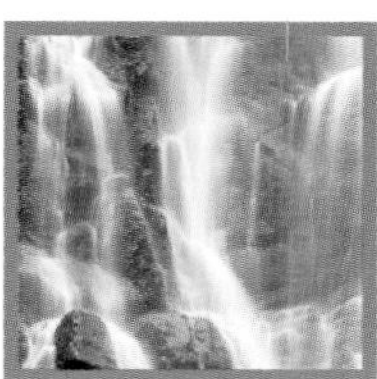

THE WATER RABBIT ★ 1903 AND 1963

Sensitive and amenable, you often go along with the flow to avoid disagreement since conflict of any kind upsets you deeply. You're friendly and easy-going with a supportive and empathetic disposition that attracts people to you, but avoid letting others take advantage of your kind, trusting nature.

THE WOOD RABBIT ★ 1915 AND 1975

People see you as a typical fence-sitter – uncertain and indecisive. However, much of this may be attributed to your inborn kindness which makes you reluctant to hurt or upset anyone. Active and generous, you're one of life's givers, always prepared to help, support and care for those in need.

THE FIRE RABBIT ★ 1927 AND 1987

Out-going, enthusiastic and bold, the Fire element makes you the most dynamic and magnetic of the Rabbit tribe. Your tendency to get-up-and-go reflects a strong adventurous streak in your nature and often leads to success in life. You can be fiery and temperamental.

THE EARTH RABBIT ★ 1939 AND 1999

Practical, serious, persistent and hard-working, the Earth influence makes you logical and level-headed as well as prudent and careful. These sterling qualities ensure trust and respect from all who know you. Domestic comfort, security and, above all, a loving partner, are absolutely essential to your well-being.

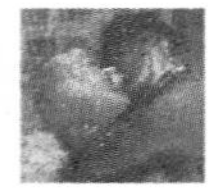

Rencontre du Soir (detail)
THEOPHILE-ALEXANDRE STEINLEN 1859–1923

Some relationships are more star-tipped than others.

Partners in Love

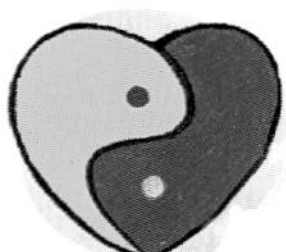

THE CHINESE are very definite about which animals are compatible with each other and which are antagonistic. So find out if you're truly suited to your partner.

RABBIT + RAT ★ *Rats rattle your nerves so if you want a quiet life it's best to give this partner a wide berth.*

RABBIT + OX ★ *This union promises a placid and contented domestic life together. In business, though, you're too laid-back to make a go of it.*

RABBIT + TIGER ★ *You're good for each other.*

RABBIT + RABBIT ★ *An easy combination between two affectionate, well-mannered, highly cultured individuals. Starred for success.*

RABBIT + DRAGON ★ *Your differences will either unite or divide you.*

RABBIT + SNAKE ★ *Deep passions make this one heck of a sexy combo!*

RABBIT + HORSE ★ *Despite conflicts you could just about put up with each other.*

LOVE PARTNERS AT A GLANCE

Rabbit with:	Tips on Togetherness	Compatibility
Rat	on different wavelengths	♥
Ox	soft and gentle	♥♥♥
Tiger	your differences weld you together	♥♥♥
Rabbit	twin souls	♥♥♥♥
Dragon	learn to give and take	♥♥
Snake	great sex	♥♥♥
Horse	difficult but achievable	♥♥
Sheep	blissful	♥♥♥♥
Monkey	heartbreak hotel	♥
Rooster	nothing in common at all	♥
Dog	rock steady	♥♥♥
Pig	shared togetherness	♥♥♥♥

COMPATIBILITY RATINGS:
♥ *conflict* ♥♥ *work at it* ♥♥♥ *strong sexual attraction* ♥♥♥♥ *heavenly!*

RABBIT + SHEEP ★ *True love, shared interests, respect, understanding. You've got the lot!*

Eiaha chipa
PAUL GAUGUIN 1848–1903

RABBIT + MONKEY ★ *It'll end in tears.*

RABBIT + ROOSTER ★ *You're opposites in almost every possible aspect you could think of.*

RABBIT + DOG ★ *You've got lots going for you here.*

RABBIT + PIG ★ *Warm, close, happy, comfortable and together. Star-tipped for enduring love.*

Christobel Finds Geraldine (detail)
WILLIAM GERSHAM COLLINGWOOD 1854–1932

Hot Dates

IF YOU'RE DATING someone for the first time, taking your partner out for a special occasion or simply wanting to re-ignite that flame of passion between you, it helps to understand what would please that person most.

RATS ★ *Wine and dine him or take her to a party. Do something on impulse... go to the races or take a flight in a hot air balloon.*

OXEN ★ *Go for a drive in the country and drop in on a stately home. Visit an art gallery or antique shops. Then have an intimate dinner à deux.*

'So glad to see you...'
COCA-COLA 1945

TIGERS ★ *Tigers thrive on excitement so go clay-pigeon shooting, Formula One racing or challenge each other to a Quasar dual. A date at the theatre will put stars in your Tiger's eyes.*

RABBITS ★ *Gentle and creative, your Rabbit date will enjoy an evening at home with some take-away food and a romantic video. Play some seductive jazz and snuggle up.*

DRAGONS ★ *Mystery and magic will thrill your Dragon date. Take in a son et lumière show or go to a carnival. Or drive to the coast and sink your toes in the sand as the sun sets.*

SNAKES ★ *Don't do anything too active – these creatures like to take life sloooowly. Hire a row-boat for a long, lazy ride down the river. Give a soothing massage, then glide into a sensual jacuzzi together.*

The Carnival
GASTON-DOIN 19/20TH CENTURY

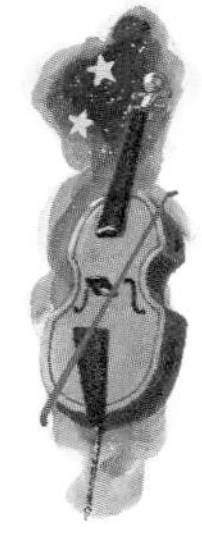

HORSES ★ *Your zany Horse gets easily bored. Take her on a mind-spinning tour of the local attractions. Surprise him with tickets to a musical show. Whatever you do, keep them guessing.*

SHEEP ★ *These folk adore the Arts so visit a museum, gallery or poetry recital. Go to a concert, the ballet, or the opera.*

MONKEYS ★ *The fantastical appeals to this partner, so go to a fancy-dress party or a masked ball, a laser light show or a sci-fi movie.*

ROOSTERS ★ *Grand gestures will impress your Rooster. Escort her to a film première or him to a formal engagement. Dressing up will place this date in seventh heaven.*

DOGS ★ *A cosy dinner will please this most unassuming of partners more than any social occasion. Chatting and story telling will ensure a close understanding.*

PIGS ★ *Arrange a slap-up meal or a lively party, or cruise through the shopping mall. Shopping is one of this partner's favourite hobbies!*

Detail from Chinese Marriage Ceremony
CHINESE PAINTING

Year of Commitment

CAN THE YEAR in which you marry (or make a firm commitment to live together) have any influence upon your marital relationship or the life you and your partner forge together? According to the Orientals, it certainly can. Whether your marriage is fiery, gentle, productive, passionate, insular or sociable doesn't so much depend on your animal nature, as on the nature of the Animal in whose year you tied the knot.

IF YOU MARRY IN A YEAR OF THE...

RAT ★ *your marriage should succeed because ventures starting now attract long-term success. Materially, you won't want and life is full of friendship.*

Marriage Feast
CHINESE PAINTING

OX ★ *your relationship will be solid and tastes conventional. Diligence will be recognized and you'll be well respected.*

TIGER ★ *you'll need plenty of humour to ride out the storms. Marrying in the Year of the Tiger is not auspicious.*

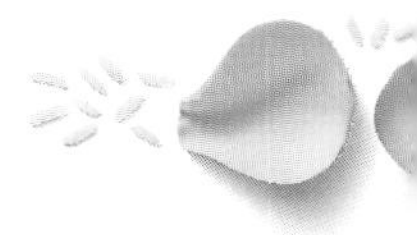

RABBIT ★ *you're wedded under the emblem of lovers. It's auspicious for a happy, carefree relationship, as neither partner wants to rock the boat.*

DRAGON ★ *you're blessed. This year is highly auspicious for luck, happiness and success.*

SNAKE ★ *it's good for romance but sexual entanglements are rife. Your relationship may seem languid, but passions run deep.*

HORSE ★ *chances are you decided to marry on the spur of the moment as the Horse year encourages impetuous behaviour. Marriage now may be volatile.*

SHEEP ★ *your family and home are blessed but watch domestic spending. Money is very easily frittered away.*

Marriage Ceremony (detail)
CHINESE PAINTING

Marriage Ceremony
CHINESE PAINTING

MONKEY ★ *married life could be unconventional. As plans go awry your lives could be full of surprises.*

ROOSTER ★ *drama characterizes your married life. Your household will run like clockwork, but bickering could strain your relationship.*

DOG ★ *it's a truly fortunate year and you can expect domestic joy. Prepare for a large family as the Dog is the sign of fertility!*

PIG ★ *it's highly auspicious and there'll be plenty of fun. Watch out for indulgence and excess.*

Detail from Chinese Marriage Ceremony
CHINESE PAINTING

TYPICAL RABBIT PLEASURES

COLOUR PREFERENCES ★ *Pale green*

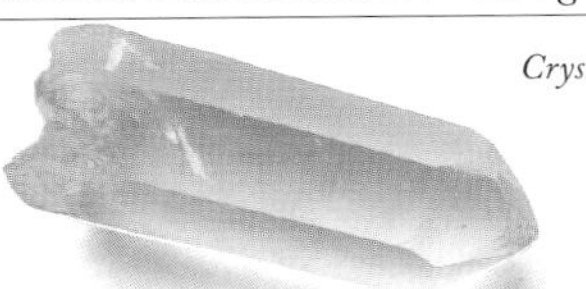

Crystal

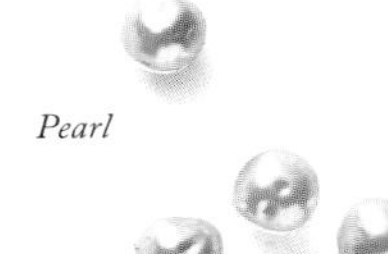

Pearl

GEMS AND STONES ★ *Pearl, crystal, emerald*

SUITABLE GIFTS ★ *A hamper from Fortnum & Mason, tapestry kit, fine wine, historical novels, original print, CDs*

HOBBIES AND PASTIMES ★ *Reading, writing, gardening, cooking, painting, rambling, sailing, golf, gossiping*

Lakeland scene, Alberta, Canada

HOLIDAY PREFERENCES ★ *Because you love your home, a vacation* chez vous *is really quite a treat. You could catch up on all those domestic jobs you've been meaning to get around to. If you must go away, choose somewhere like Florence, Paris or Rhodes.*

COUNTRIES LINKED WITH THE RABBIT ★ *Holland, Belgium, Wales, Canada, Switzerland*

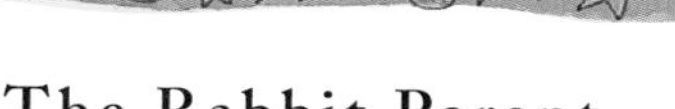

The Rabbit Parent

THE CHINESE SAY THE RABBIT is the sign of fertility and many Rabbit-born individuals do have large families. But however many children you choose to have, a happy family life is central to your scheme of things. Loyal and supportive, you're very protective towards your young, if a little over-possessive of them too. When they're little you'll dress them in stylish clothes and insist on politeness. Because you find squabbles disagreeable, you're likely to give in to their demands for the sake of a quiet life.

PATIENCE

With your deeply caring instinct you nurse your little ones tenderly and patiently through all their childhood illnesses. As they grow, you provide wise counsel to guide them through their lives.

THE RABBIT HABITAT

You have an intense love for your home. Security and comfort are important since you need to feel snug as a bug in a rug. At the top of the list are style and elegance because living in uncongenial surroundings makes you depressed. Your home will be tastefully furnished, and for you less is definitely more. With your artistic skills you create a graceful environment, filled with pretty things or with the best antiques you can afford. Green is your colour, so think of accenting your décor with eau-de-nil, jade or sage to produce that air of cool, chic refinement that characterizes your good taste.

Animal Babies

FOR SOME parents, their children's personalities harmonize perfectly with their own. Others find that no matter how much they may love their offspring they're just not on the same wavelength. Our children arrive with their characters already well formed and, according to Chinese philosophy, shaped by the influence of their Animal Year. So you should be mindful of the year in which you conceive.

BABIES BORN IN THE YEAR OF THE...

RAT ★ *love being cuddled. They keep on the go – so give them plenty of rest. Later they enjoy collecting things.*

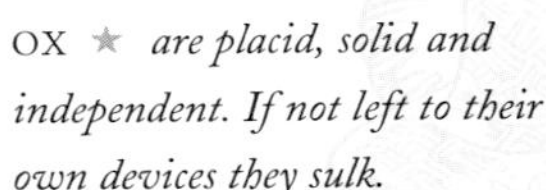

OX ★ *are placid, solid and independent. If not left to their own devices they sulk.*

TIGER ★ *are happy and endearing. As children, they have irrepressible energy. Boys are sporty and girls tom-boys.*

RABBIT ★ *are sensitive and strongly bonded to their mother. They need stability to thrive.*

DRAGON ★ *are independent and imaginative from the start. Encourage any interest that will allow their talents to flourish.*

SNAKE ★ *have great charm. They are slow starters so may need help with school work. Teach them to express feelings.*

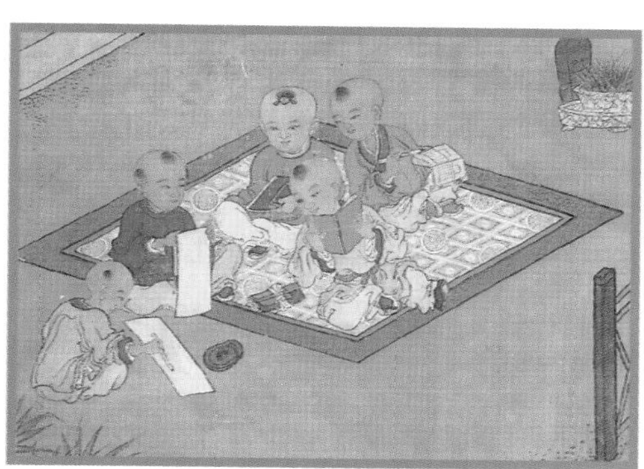

One Hundred Children Scroll
ANON, MING PERIOD

HORSE ★ *will burble away contentedly for hours. Talking starts early and they excel in languages.*

SHEEP ★ *are placid, well-behaved and respectful. They are family-oriented and never stray too far from home.*

MONKEY ★ *take an insatiable interest in everything. With agile minds they're quick to learn. They're good-humoured but mischievous!*

ROOSTER ★ *are sociable. Bright and vivacious, their strong adventurous streak best shows itself on a sports field.*

DOG ★ *are cute and cuddly. Easily pleased, they are content just pottering around the house amusing themselves for hours. Common sense is their greatest virtue.*

PIG ★ *are affectionate and friendly. Well-balanced, self-confident children, they're happy-go-lucky and laid-back. They are popular with friends.*

Health, Wealth and Worldly Affairs

DESPITE THE FACT that Rabbit folk are said to be blessed with longevity you do have a delicate constitution. Physiologically you're prone to allergies and stomach ailments. Psychologically you're sensitive and suffer under adverse living conditions or emotional pressure of any kind. A notorious love of creature comforts may mean you don't exercise enough. Make a point of getting out into the fresh air as a regular part of a healthy routine.

CAREER

The greatest asset you bring to any occupation is your depth of psychological understanding. This, coupled with excellent business acumen, makes you successful in commercial occupations. But medicine and the Arts are the occupations tailor-made for Rabbits. Counselling or psychotherapy would be ideal.

Teaching is an ideal Rabbit occupation.

You're not made for dirty physical work, so you're much more likely to be found in professions where you can use your negotiating and man-management skills. That's why the Diplomatic Corps, PR and teaching are for you.

Meissen porcelain depicting a Chinese scene
C. 1723

With your sense of beauty and artistic inclinations, many of you find your niche in music, literature or the Arts. Joining an orchestra, writing historical novels, acting, publishing are areas in which you excel.

FINANCES

Though financially careful and clever, you tend to be fairly lucky. Your chic appearance and elegant home suggest affluence and much of your money is tied up in your possessions and your house. A terrific nose for genuine antiques ensures some wise investments.

FRIENDSHIPS

Rabbits have a strong urge to identify themselves with a group, so you may well belong to a club or association, which provides an excellent source of like-minded individuals. You're a sympathetic friend, a terrific shoulder to cry on and a wise counsellor. There's nothing you enjoy better than a gossip with your pals!

RABBITS MAKE EXCELLENT:

★ Therapists ★ Psychiatrists ★ Doctors ★ Masseurs ★
★ Ophthalmologists ★ Herbalists ★ Solicitors ★ Judges ★
★ Diplomats ★ Campaigners ★ Teachers ★ Writers ★
★ Publishers ★ Designers ★ Actors ★ Musicians ★
★ Administrators ★ Welfare workers ★ PR agents ★
★ Fashion designers ★ Beauticians ★

兔

East Meets West

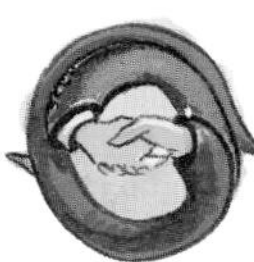

COMBINE YOUR Oriental Animal sign with your Western Zodiac birth sign to form a deeper and richer understanding of your character and personality.

ARIES RABBIT ★ *Your constant search for new opportunities means many changes of direction. Career-wise you are suited to creative occupations. In love, you're not the most constant of Rabbits.*

TAUREAN RABBIT ★ *Top-of-the-list for you are creature comforts, followed by security and the need to live and work in refined environments. Emotionally, you keep your feet on the ground.*

GEMINI RABBIT ★ *Chatty and sociable, a low boredom threshold means you need stimulation. You enjoy a gossip but you can be the soul of discretion. An intelligent partner makes a good match, but you can be selfish.*

CANCERIAN RABBIT ★ *For you, home is where the heart is. Romantic, you have a traditional attitude to love and marriage. You need a solid partner by your side who will share your devotion to family and home.*

LEONINE RABBIT ★ *Your charismatic personality makes you popular, so there's never a shortage of suitors. Refined and accomplished, your ideal partner must be elegant with good manners.*

VIRGO RABBIT ★ *You're practical and capable, and can turn your hand to anything. At home you like everything to be neat and orderly, at work you're efficient and organized. In relationships, you're a bit too self-sacrificing.*

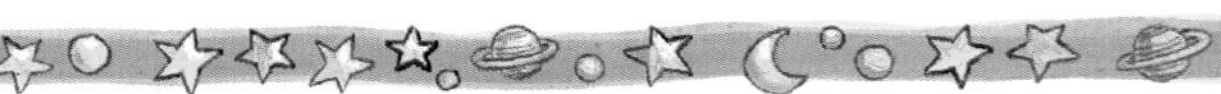

LIBRAN RABBIT

★ *Charming, suave and sophisticated, you're a wonderful, colourful social butterfly with manners that are delicate and refined. You believe in the best of all possible worlds and go through life completely in love with love.*

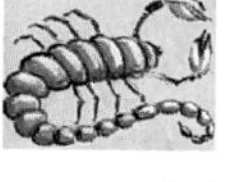

SCORPIO RABBIT

★ *In work as well as romance, you play your cards close to your chest. Emotionally, you're passionate and very intense. Woe betide anyone who toys with your volatile affections – you have an unforgiving nature and a deadly sting in your tail!*

SAGITTARIAN RABBIT

★ *You're talented, sexy and terrific fun to be with but a bit of a rover. For you, relationships need to be fluid. Ideally, a suitable partner would be one who is happy to take over domestic control, leaving you free to pursue your own aspirations.*

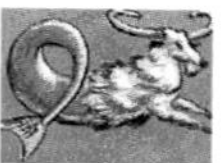

CAPRICORN RABBIT

★ *Ambitious, you work hard in order to attain the high standards of living to which you aspire. Although loving, you tend not to be demonstrative in your affections. Only a hard-working partner will be deemed worthy of your attentions.*

AQUARIAN RABBIT

★ *Because this is the sign of the intellect, the acquisition of knowledge will certainly be central to your life. Accordingly, the ideal partner is someone who is intelligent and articulate and who enjoys endless amusing, informative discussions.*

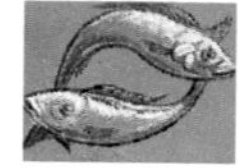

PISCEAN RABBIT

★ *Mix sensitivity with astuteness, idealism with adroitness and kindness with finesse and you can see what a complex creature you are. You look at love through rose-coloured spectacles but your feet are firmly on the ground.*

FAMOUS RABBITS

Cary Grant

Tina Turner

Queen Victoria

Joseph Stalin

Albert Einstein

Fidel Castro

Frank Sinatra

Queen Victoria ★ Stalin ★ Cary Grant
Evelyn Waugh ★ Walt Whitman ★ Andy Warhol
Cecil Beaton ★ Marie Curie
Albert Einstein ★ Cary Grant
Ingrid Bergman ★ Dr Benjamin Spock
Fidel Castro ★ David Frost ★ John Cleese
Bob Hope ★ George Michael ★ Roger Moore
Neil Simon ★ Frank Sinatra ★ Tina Turner
Whitney Houston ★ John Hurt

Ingrid Bergman

The Rabbit Year in Focus

SANDWICHED BETWEEN TWO of the most turbulent and unpredictable Animal signs, the year of the Rabbit may be likened to the eye of the storm. This is a time of recuperation, a year in which to soothe your nerves and catch your breath.

DIPLOMATIC RELATIONS

Indeed, this is not a year to force issues, all efforts falling upon stony ground and melting in the heat of the sun. But it is a time for negotiation, for diplomatic relations and for reaching settlements and mutual agreements.

FOCUS ON WOMEN

The year of the Rabbit focuses on women and their interests: children and the family, food and welfare, home and domestic security become salient issues. Medical advances will be made and the Arts will be a prominent feature on the agenda.

The Rabbit Year is a year for reaching agreements.

ACTIVITIES ASSOCIATED WITH THE YEAR OF THE RABBIT

The discovery, invention, patenting, marketing, occurrence or manufacturing of: the first talking movie, theory of relativity, quasars, nylon stockings, DDT, first woman to climb Everest, Entente Cordiale, advances in dental treatment, New York's World Fair and the Festival of Britain.

Your Rabbit Fortunes for the Next 12 Years

1996 MARKS THE BEGINNING of a new 12-year cycle in the Chinese calendar. How your relationships and worldly prospects fare will depend on the influence of each Animal year in turn.

1996 YEAR OF THE RAT *19 Feb 1996 – 6 Feb 1997*

The high-octane pulse of the Rat Year is not conducive to your need for a calm existence, so 1996 may be unsettling for you. On the whole an up-hill struggle, especially financially, though some progress is made.

YEAR TREND: GIVE NEW PROJECTS THE GO-AHEAD

1997 YEAR OF THE OX *7 Feb 1997 – 27 Jan 1998*

Domestic, rather than occupational, matters are aspected for you during an Oxen Year. The even pace of 1997 will be more to your liking and encourage you to spend time with friends and loved ones.

YEAR TREND: BUY, SELL OR IMPROVE YOUR HOME

1998 YEAR OF THE TIGER *28 Jan 1998 – 15 Feb 1999*

Despite the dramatic turn of events so characteristic of Tiger Years, you should find yourself prospering now. It's an excellent time to put plans and projects into operation but read the small print carefully!

YEAR TREND: LAY DOWN FUTURE FOUNDATIONS

1999 YEAR OF THE RABBIT *16 Feb 1999 – 4 Feb 2000*

A high-profile year for you in which everything you touch seems to turn to gold. Physically, you feel on top form, work is successful and past efforts rewarded. Romance blossoms and love bring happiness.

YEAR TREND: REVIVING, RESTORING, REUNITING

2000 YEAR OF THE DRAGON *5 Feb 2000 – 23 Jan 2001*

Dragon Years can be tricky for Rabbits so you may find a few hurdles need to be negotiated during 2000. You'll need to put in considerable overtime in all spheres of your life in order to make any progress now.

YEAR TREND: BEWARE GET-RICH-QUICK SCHEMES

Dragon years can be hard-going.

2001 YEAR OF THE SNAKE *24 Jan 2001 – 11 Feb 2002*

Snake Years are generally auspicious for Rabbits so the trends in 2001 could well be in your favour. However, new romantic liaisons may promise much but could leave you in a somewhat embarrassing situation.

YEAR TREND: DON'T JUDGE A BOOK BY ITS COVER!

2002 YEAR OF THE HORSE *12 Feb 2002 – 31 Jan 2003*

Socially, 2002 is likely to be a busy year when you will be extending your network of contacts. New acquaintances could prove fortunate in helping you achieve your aims. Encounters lead to romance.

YEAR TREND: LOVE IS BITTER-SWEET

2003 YEAR OF THE SHEEP *1 Feb 2003 – 21 Jan 2004*

Domestically and emotionally, 2003 will prove most satisfying for you. Existing relationships are harmonious while singletons are likely to find true love now. Social life is buzzing and occupational matters rewarding.

YEAR TREND: GO FOR A NEW IMAGE

2004 YEAR OF THE MONKEY *22 Jan 2004 – 8 Feb 2005*

This is a year of mixed blessings for you when fortune smiles on your love life but tends to hinder your progress at work. Finances especially could become very strained and you're advised to be prudent over spending.

YEAR TREND: DON'T EXCEED YOUR LIMITS

Concentrate on domestic pleasures.

2005 YEAR OF THE ROOSTER *9 Feb 2005 – 28 Jan 2006*

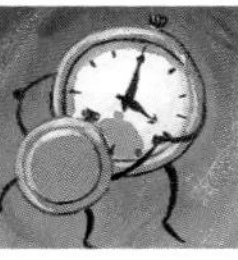

Keeping a low profile throughout 2005 is the best way for you to avoid the pitfalls and frustrations you usually encounter in a Rooster Year. Concentrate on domestic pleasures and on enjoying quality time with your loved ones.

YEAR TREND: KEEP ASPIRATIONS MODEST

2006 YEAR OF THE DOG *29 Jan 2006 – 17 Feb 2007*

Dog Years are times in which you can make up lost ground. With no major hurdles either at work or in romance, you should make steady progress. Intimate and business partners are supportive to your aims.

YEAR TREND: SET YOUR SIGHTS HIGH

2007 YEAR OF THE PIG *18 Feb 2007 – 6 Feb 2008*

Relax and let your hair down this year. Join a club, take up a new hobby, accept all invitations, travel, expand your horizons. Progress at work is moderate but love makes up for everything. Marriage now is highly auspicious.

YEAR TREND: ROMANCE IS IN THE AIR

PICTURE CREDITS

AKG Berlin/Erich Lessing: pp.24L, 34
AKG London: pp.21, 25L, 26, 27B
e. t. archive
British Museum: pp.33T;
Victoria & Albert Museum: 28, 29,
Fine Art Photographic Library Ltd:
pp.25R, 27T, 32-3
Horizon/Robert Estall: p.30
Hulton Deutsch Collection: p.38
(Bergman, Einstein, Grant,
Queen Victoria, Stalin)
Images Colour Library:
pp.8, 22T & B, 23
Kobal Collection: p.38 (Sinatra)
Rex Features: p.38 (Castro/Sipa-Press,
Turner)